From Cross Purposes to Cooperation

From Cross Purposes to Cooperation

The Ten Factors that Unify a Cross-Functional Team

Emilio De Lia and Ellen Fredericks

iUniverse, Inc.
New York Lincoln Shanghai

From Cross Purposes to Cooperation
The Ten Factors that Unify a Cross-Functional Team

iUniverse books may be ordered through booksellers or by contacting:

iUniverse
2021 Pine Lake Road, Suite 100
Lincoln, NE 68512
www.iuniverse.com
1-800-Authors (1-800-288-4677)

ISBN-13: 978-0-595-36835-8 (pbk)
ISBN-13: 978-0-595-81248-6 (ebk)
ISBN-10: 0-595-36835-2 (pbk)
ISBN-10: 0-595-81248-1 (ebk)

Printed in the United States of America

A special thank you to our editor, Susan Meigs, and our photographer, Ruby Naylor.

CONTENTS

INTRODUCTION

THE CROSS-FUNCTIONAL TEAM:
A PARADIGM OF UNITY AND HOW TO CREATE IT

Let's face it. Creating a successful team can be a tough challenge even in the best of circumstances. Today's fast-paced business and global workforce increase the challenge, as time frames are compressed and complexity grows due to mergers, acquisitions, and downsizings.

Gone are the days when new products, technical problems, or cost reductions could be tackled by individuals from the same functional area, or using the old linking approaches between functional groups. More and more we find companies creating cross-functional teams in response. Even with the special challenges they present, cross-functional teams are more adept at overcoming organizational barriers, creating new solutions, and managing to achieve extraordinary value in a short time frame.

By definition, a cross-functional team brings together members from different functional areas, such as marketing, finance, sales, and operations, each with its own chain of command. Typically a cross-functional team has a designated sponsor and leader. A unified cross-functional team bridges and solves the issues that put functional organizations at cross purposes. Cross-functional teams are formed for a variety of specific purposes, such as:

- to bring products to market or to profitability more quickly
- to find quick cost-reduction opportunities
- to jumpstart revenue or market-share growth
- to improve the quality of operations and results
- to discover better ways of doing business that will serve the company or customer
- to find revenue, cost, and operational synergies within product lines
- to integrate product lines as a result of a downsizing, reorganization, or merger/acquisition
- to respond to a competitor's latest move, and
- to prepare more comprehensive and timely business plans and forecasts.

Cross-functional teams have the potential to deliver results that a team in "business as usual" mode could not. But without acknowledging and managing the uniqueness of a cross-functional team structure, many do not achieve success. While cross-functional teams face many of the same issues functional teams do, there are other complexities and dynamics to consider:

- competing functional area goals that conflict with the team's purpose
- team members who are not full time to the team yet are expected to participate fully
- unclear sponsorship and ownership for the team and its goals
- a lack of resources from each functional area represented on the team

- geographic and time zone differences

- compressed time frames to become effective and to deliver the result

- few, if any, formal or informal company-wide supporting structures

- no pre-existing team identity to establish credibility and authority

These complexities are challenges your team must overcome to be successful. This book is designed to help you do just that. Having managed many cross-functional teams ourselves, we examine the factors that are critical to success, and, drawing on our experience, lay out a simple plan for creating a high-performing team.

High-performing teams are unified in their identity, purpose, and plan. Since a cross-functional team is often up against short time frames, the team must quickly and successfully address the challenge of ten critical unity factors:

The Customer Factor: What is the team's relationship to its customers?

The Engagement Factor: Does the team engage its members to the level necessary for the team to succeed?

The Identity Factor: How strong is the team's identity?

The Behavior Factor: Does the team demonstrate constructive norms and behaviors?

The Plan Factor: Does the team have a clearly defined plan of action that the members believe in?

The Process Factor: How effectively does the team communicate and make decisions?

The Function Factor: How are the team's efforts integrated into the functional organizations?

The Feedback Factor: How is performance evaluated and rewarded?

The Responsibility Factor: What level of responsibility and commitment do members of the team demonstrate?

The Self-Interest Factor: Do team members see personal advantages to working on the team?

Examining these ten success factors will help you evaluate your cross-functional team. You will identify your vulnerabilities, compare yourselves to a high-performing team, and create a plan to capitalize on what is working and improve what is not. It's simple and practical. As a result, you will see your overall team performance and results soar.

How To Use This Book

This book is designed so you, team leaders and team members, can easily and accurately evaluate if your team is working in a unified manner or at cross purposes. Following our approach of "first evaluate, then take action," this book leads you through a two-step process.

The first step is to assess your team's potential using the TRUID Cross-Functional Team Scorecard. Your responses to the scorecard's twenty-five statements will gauge your team's potential by considering ten factors that we have found to be critical to a cross-functional team's success. When you have completed the scoring guide, you will be able to readily identify which of the ten factors you need to look at more closely. In this second step, you examine how each factor affects performance, how your team stacks up, and, most important, what action you can take.

It's as simple as that. The process for evaluating and taking action is laid out for you. With clear directions, you can pinpoint opportunities and take focused action.

The TRUID Cross-Functional Team Scorecard

The scorecard is a simple questionnaire designed to be used by a single individual, either the team leader or a team member, or by the entire team.

TRUID Cross Functional Team Scorecard

These statements will help your team determine the level at which it is functioning as a team. The term "functional" refers to the home organization which a member comes from and represents on the team. Please pick a number from the scale to show how much you agree or disagree with each statement and mark it in the space to the right of the statement.

Scale
4 Agree
3 Somewhat Agree
2 Somewhat Disagree
1 Disagree

I know who the customers of this team are. ____ 1

This team is focused on the needs of our customers. ____ 2

The team engages all its members. ____ 3

I am satisfied with how the team engages my talents and skills. ____ 4

I identify with and am proud of what this team stands for. ____ 5

We have a strong sense of identity on this team. ____ 6

I respect the norms and behaviors by which this team works ____ 7

The team corrects behaviors that are destructive. ____ 8

I believe that the right people are on the team. ____ 9

The team has a clear plan that will get us to our goals. ____ 10

I know how my roles and responsibilities fit into the team's plan. ____ 11

I am committed to the purpose and goals of the team. ____ 12

I see a high level of truthfulness and openness from other members of the team. _____ 13

The team has effective ways of communicating. _____ 14

The team has an effective decision making process backed by functional management. _____ 15

My functional management is aligned with my roles and responsibilities for the team. _____ 16

My functional budget includes the needs of the team. _____ 17

My functional management will acknowledge and reward my work for the team. _____ 18

The team evaluates its performance regularly. _____ 19

I get regular feedback from the team on my performance. _____ 20

Team members deliver on their responsibilities to the team. _____ 21

I see a high level of commitment from the other members of the team. _____ 22

I am committed to this team. _____ 23

I value the personal payoffs I get from being on this team. _____ 24

I am proud of my contribution to this team. _____ 25

Total   _____

Steps for Individual Use

1. Rate the twenty-five statements according to the instructions at the top of the scorecard on page **6**.

2. Transcribe your answers into the scoring guide on page **10**.

3. Use the scoring guide to determine which statements show your team's strengths or weaknesses.

4. Select the factors you want to study further.

Steps for Team Use

1. Distribute copies of the scorecard on pages **6 and 7** to all of the team members and ask them to complete it and return it to you by a specified date. (You can instruct them either to identify their scorecards or to return them anonymously.)

2. Compile the members' ratings for each statement and average them. (Add the ratings for each statement and divide by the number of responding members.)

3. Enter the average for each statement on the appropriate line on the scoring guide on page **10**.

4. Use the scoring guide to determine which statements show your team's strengths or weaknesses.

5. Select the factors you want to study further yourself and that you want your team to address.

Evaluating Your Results—The Scoring Guide

Your score on each statement ranks your perception of your team's strength or weakness. When you average the ratings given by all the members on your team, you have an even more powerful indicator. Here's how to interpret your scores:

From 3.5 to 4.0: Your team is highly unified and highly functioning.

From 3.0 to 3.5: Your team is unified and adequately functioning.

From 2.0 to 3.0: Your team is in jeopardy.

Below 2.0: Your team is working at cross purposes.

The scorecard's statements are then mapped onto the Ten Success Factors to identify those that are most significant for your team. Transcribe your scores into the appropriate spaces below. Each statement is cross-referenced to a discussion in the text of each success factor and how it can affect results.

When you turn to our analysis of each factor, you will be asked to write down what you observe about your team. *Do this important step. It will pay-off when selecting actions to take.* After reading our comments, you will choose from a checklist of recommended actions. You can track your progress by returning to check off those you have completed.

We recommend taking the time to review all the factors, whether your scores were high or low. Often performance is improved by making your strengths even stronger. Good Luck and enjoy your more unified and higher performing team!

The Scoring Guide

Write your score for each statement in the space provided.

The **Customer Factor:** Statements 1____ and 2____ (*see page 11*)

The **Engagement Factor:** Statements 3____ and 4____ (*see page 16*)

The **Identity Factor:** Statements 5____ and 6____ (*see page 20*)

The **Behavior Factor:** Statements 7____, 8____, and 9____ (*see page 25*)

The **Plan Factor:** Statements 10____, 11____, and 12____ (*see page 32*)

The **Process Factor:** Statements 13____, 14____, and 15____ (*see page 36*)

The **Functional Factor:** Statements 16____, 17____, and 18____ (*see page 42*)

The **Feedback Factor:** Statements 19____ and 20____ (*see page 46*)

The **Responsibility Factor:** Statements 21____, 22____, and 23____ (*see page 50*)

The **Self-Interest Factor:** Statements 24____ and 25____ (*see page 55*)

THE CUSTOMER FACTOR

WHAT IS THE TEAM'S RELATIONSHIP TO ITS CUSTOMERS?

What a member of a high-performing team observes:
  I know who the customers of this team are.
  This team is focused on the needs of our customers.

Write observations about your team:

The Coach's Perspective

Too often teams operate without a complete connection to their customers. A team's success is jeopardized if it does not know who its real customer is or what makes its output valuable to the customer.

Your team's customers can be internal or external. They can be end customers who purchase the company's goods and services, or intermediates, such as suppliers or channels. In some rare cases the customer could be the sponsor of the team. But in all cases, you must identify the prime recipients for the benefits your team produces.

High-functioning teams are closely bound to their customer. The team knows and understands the customer well. The customer is represented on the team and cared for. The team develops its identity, purpose, and plan by focusing on delivering the greatest value it can to this customer. The delivery of this value becomes a rallying point for the functional groups supporting the team. Finally, the team determines its success by evaluating the value it produces for its customers.

Your team must design and implement ways to include and care for the customer. If there is a single customer, you can arrange for their actual participation. For example, in identifying needs you can interview the customer to obtain their needs. Once the needs are documented, you can ask the customer to comment on your understanding. More often, the customer is a large diverse group. Seek out information about the group. You will need to initiate actions to gather sufficient reliable information if it is not available.

Identifying Your Customer Types

Different types of customers present different challenges and require different responses. When the customer is the end customer—the purchaser of the firm's goods or services—the team is challenged to understand the customer's requirements sufficiently so that when the team produces its results, there will indeed be purchasers. The team can turn to the marketing group, if there is one, or to the sales group for the required expertise. It is best to have representatives from one of these two groups on the team. Very often, the customer requirements have already been defined and the information can be readily used. If customer requirements have not been identified by Marketing or Sales, the team will need direct input from customers, which is always valuable. This can be pursued through interviews or questionnaires designed by the team. Be sure to continue to take the customer's pulse as the project progresses. Requirements can change in the dynamic competitive environment most firms face.

Closely related to the end customer are customer intermediaries—the distributors, wholesalers, and retailers known as channels. When channels are the team's customer, the team has a special challenge to create results that provide value or advantages for both their own firm and the channel. The channel must be represented on the team either directly or through an internal group that has interface responsibility. Because value is realized by both the firm and the channel only when products or services are sold to the end customer, the end customer's requirements must also be understood. When your information and expertise are coming from both the channel and internal sources, any differences must be resolved. The team should check in frequently with the channel as things progress.

A third category of customer is the supplier. The most successful approach to handling suppliers is to design their role or their inputs into the overall process. Ensuring a tight integration is therefore essential for the cross-functional team. The first action to take is to ensure that the appropriate internal groups who interface with the supplier are on the team. Next, the team should assess the supplier's requirements and any internal requirements and determine how the two mesh. The team should verify its thinking with the supplier. During development, the team should check in with the supplier to ensure that what is being developed will indeed achieve the desired results.

The final type of customer we will consider is the internal customer, who, surprisingly, sometimes can be the most challenging. The simplest approach is to have the internal customer on the team. This representative should provide a clear and straightforward source of requirements and testing. Difficulties, however, can arise if the internal customer is a complex organization or has a confusing chain of command, so that no one person can speak with authority. If the group is complex, representatives of the different subgroups may need to be added. When this is done, it is important to establish how disagreements or trade-offs will be decided; otherwise road blocks and failure can be expected. It will become more and more difficult for the team to move ahead if authority is unclear.

Cross-functional teams sometimes mistake other stakeholders, such as participating functional groups, for the customer. This confusion can result if the team must continually justify its efforts because it is competing for resources with functional needs. While it is helpful to treat other stakeholders like customers, the value of your team is determined by how well your ultimate customer is served.

Select actions from the list below that you want your team to act on. Add other actions as you see necessary.

Success Factor Actions:

	YES	NO	DONE
Identify the customer(s) of your team.	☐	☐	☐
Determine how the customer will be represented.	☐	☐	☐
Gather existing customer intelligence.	☐	☐	☐
Seek out additional information if required.	☐	☐	☐
Determine customer needs to be addressed by your team.	☐	☐	☐
Verify that your plan of action meets customer needs.	☐	☐	☐
Other:			
	☐	☐	☐
	☐	☐	☐

THE ENGAGEMENT FACTOR

DOES THE TEAM ENGAGE ITS MEMBERS TO THE LEVEL
NECESSARY FOR THE TEAM TO SUCCEED?

What a member of a high-performing team observes:
> *I am satisfied with how the team engages my talents and strengths.*
> *The team engages all its members.*

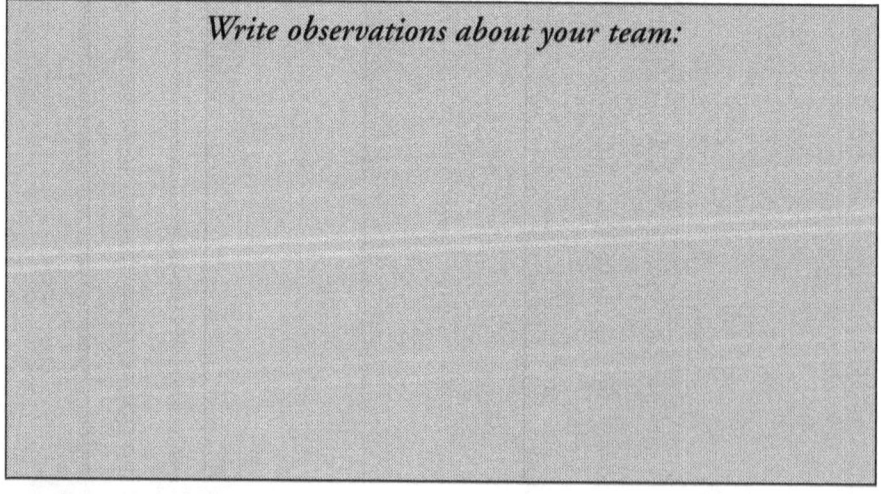

Write observations about your team:

The Coach's Perspective

Engaged people outperform unengaged people. The cross-functional team must engage its members very quickly, often while competing with its members' regular assignments for their attention.

A lack of engagement tends to characterize dysfunctional teams. It is costly. Unengaged people don't care about the goals and outcomes of the team. They remain distant and often passive, only doing what is minimally expected. Even when a team is well off track and headed for a train wreck, unengaged members will just watch it happen.

The Challenge of Engagement

A cross-functional team's initial challenge, then, is to engage its people quickly and intensely. How do you do so? In the list below we have compiled the findings of The Gallup Organization, which has studied this question extensively.

Teams create engagement when they:

- make clear right away what is expected of members,
- see to it that members have what they need to do their work,
- find out members' strengths and make sure they get to do what they do best
- recognize and praise individual members' contributions,
- offer encouragement,
- make members' opinions count in decisions,
- recognize members early on and often when they demonstrate engagement,
- create relationships that go deeper than the work, and
- give members opportunities to experience personal growth.

Cross-functional teams can meet this challenge and create engagement when they help team members:

- feel part of the team and connected to the other members *(the Identity Factor),*

- understand how they, the members, will make a contribution to the team and ultimately to the customer *(the Plan Factor),*

- get recognition from the team and from their home functional organization *(the Feedback Factor),*

- participate in the decisions of the team *(the Process Factor),*

- get a personal payoff from being part of the team *(the Self-Interest Factor),* and

- use their talents and strengths to do what they do *best (the Self-Interest Factor).*

Often cross-functional teams make the mistake of not taking the time to do what is necessary to create engagement. Early on, when your team is forming, take the time to find out what challenges members face by coming onto the team, what they most enjoy doing, and how they see themselves contributing to the team. Sharing each other's strengths and talents is a great way to increase productivity, trust, and morale. To increase engagement, pay attention to building relationships among team members. On high-functioning teams, members learn about and are responsive to each other.

Select actions from the list below that you want your team to act on. Add other actions as you see necessary.

Success Factor Actions:

	YES	NO	DONE
Tell team members that their engagement is desired.	☐	☐	☐
Be sure members get to do what they do best.	☐	☐	☐
Foster mutual encouragement among members.	☐	☐	☐
Recognize individuals when they act with engagement.	☐	☐	☐
Establish norms to promote relationship-building among team members.	☐	☐	☐
Other:			
	☐	☐	☐
	☐	☐	☐

THE IDENTITY FACTOR

HOW STRONG IS THE TEAM'S IDENTITY?

What a member of a high-performing team observes:
   I identify with and am proud of what this team stands for.
   We have a strong sense of identity on this team.

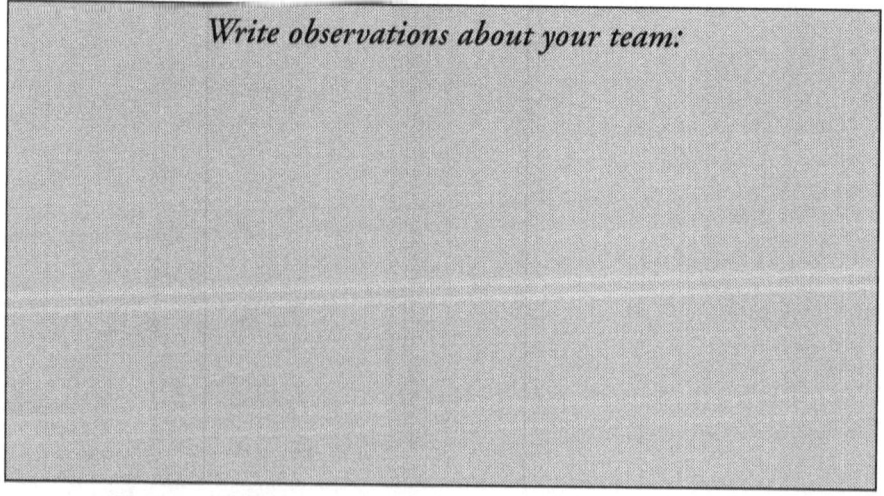

Write observations about your team:

The Coach's Perspective

Identity is who your team uniquely is. A strong team has an identity tied to the unique value the team creates for its customers and its company. A team's identity is shared by its members and recognized by others. It asserts the team's purpose and helps align the members' values and aspirations. Low-functioning teams frequently lack a sense of unique or strong identity.

Because members normally come to a team with an identity affiliated to their functional organization, the challenge is for you to create a new identity that all members can embrace. This allows members to hold in balance both their identity as part of the functional organization and as part of your team.

Choosing an Identity

What identities can teams create? It is important that the identity be a powerful rallying point for members and that it clarify the unique value the team will create. Identity is more than the name of the team. The identity embodies values and aspirations that make the team members proud. Members should see what is important to them reflected in their identity. How does the identity become more than a name? Identity comes alive through consistent values and behaviors of the team. The team's identity takes on meaning and defining characteristics through the values and behaviors the team demonstrates in the conduct of its business.

Probably the most common identity for a cross-functional team to have is one centered on the team's main goal or product, such as the New Widget Team, the Purchase Order System Team, or the Cost Reduction Team. This type of identity is especially appropriate when the team has a very difficult and/or critically important goal. Choosing this type of identity communicates the importance of committing to and achieving the goal the team takes on. Values and behaviors consistent with this type of identity include having a singular focus, striving to achieve intermediate and final goals at any cost, and dedicating all one's efforts to the task.

Another common type of identity is one that focuses on serving the customer. This identity is typically used when the customer of the team is indeed the end customer of the firm, the purchaser of its goods or services. Examples include the High End Customer Team and the Small Business Solution Team. This type of identity communicates a tight alignment with the customer and dedication to the customer's needs. Consistent behaviors would include sustaining in-depth interaction with the customer, encouraging customer participation on the team, using customers to pilot the results of the team, and measuring team success with customer statistics.

A third identity type that is often used is the expert team. These identities are built on a special expertise the team possesses. Examples are the Super charger Team, the Legal Team, and the Personnel Team. This type of identity works especially well when a group of specialists from different parts of the company are brought together to apply their concentrated know-how to a particular task. It follows that the defining behavior on such teams is the application of their expertise.

There are other types of team identities that are less common but are worth considering. We will briefly mention two. Team identity can be based on a new or high standard the team is trying to achieve, such as the Zero Defect Team or the Total Satisfaction Team. This identity is relevant when the standard is intended not as a single goal but as a guiding principle for continuous improvement. The team builds this identity by applying the standard to themselves and demonstrating how it can be achieved. And finally, team identity can come from the larger group that the team represents, such as The Northwest Region Improvement Team and the Engineering Department Process Team. This type of identity is particularly effective when the larger group itself is the customer. The team displays its identity when its actions continually benefit the larger group. Its central value is that the benefit of the whole is more valuable than that of individual sections.

Communicating Your Identity

Once your team has an identity, communicating it is particularly important, especially when a cross-functional team has just been brought together. Through team identity, you establish credibility and authority. Your team can then more easily plug into existing formal or informal company-wide support networks. It is easier to get things done and to be heard.

Creating a team identity generates greater passion and engagement. As your members integrate their identities, values, abilities, and aspirations, the team forms an identity greater than each individual member. People feel as if they belong, yet each individual's uniqueness is maximized as their abilities are tapped and the team coalesces.

Identity provides cohesiveness over time, uniting your members and directing their actions. It becomes a compass to keep your team focused on delivering the greatest value to your customers.

Select actions from the list below that you want your team to act on. Add other actions as you see necessary.

Success Factor Actions:	YES	NO	DONE
Describe the unique characteristics of your team.	☐	☐	☐
Describe the unique value that your team can create.	☐	☐	☐
Identify what is important and valued by team members.	☐	☐	☐
Determine an identity your team will rally to.	☐	☐	☐
Communicate your team's identity to others.	☐	☐	☐
Other:			
	☐	☐	☐
	☐	☐	☐

THE BEHAVIOR FACTOR

What a member of a high-performing team observes:
   I respect the norms and behaviors by which this team works.
   The team corrects behaviors that are destructive.
   I believe that the right people are on the team.

Write observations about your team:

The Coach's Perspective

Often teams succeed or fail for what seem to be invisible reasons. The talent was right. The purpose was solid. The leader was experienced. However, the team failed to produce. Though the cause of the failure appears elusive it really was out in the open all the time. It boils down to the way members behaved and the undermining effects of attitudes that were allowed to develop.

Dysfunctional teams not only exhibit bad behavior, but worse, they neglect to deal with or stop dysfunctional behavior, for various reasons:

- The team may not have established norms.
- Members may not be clear about the norms by which the team operates.
- The team may treat dysfunctional behavior inconsistently, which reinforces bad behavior.
- It may have conflicting norms, such as "tell the truth but don't deliver bad news."

Yet many of the common behaviors that are destructive to a team are also symptoms. Once they are recognized, they can be dealt with accordingly.

Typical Dysfunctional Behaviors

Gossip

Talking about other team members in an unfavorable way or making assumptions about the team that may not be true is one of the most damaging behaviors for a team. Gossip is often a signal that communication may be lacking or is too erratic. When people don't get their questions answered or feel safe enough to ask directly, they gossip. And what people don't know, they make up. The bottom line is it undermines trust. Work on creating an environment that promotes trust and open and honest communication. You may also need to increase communication among team members, whether through additional formal meetings or in one-on-one discussions.

Guarded conversations

When people are guarded, they watch what they say, limiting input and feedback. This is another sign that people feel insecure or suspicious. When people don't feel safe, they stay guarded in what they are willing to share. Check in with members of the team to see what is creating the perception of a lack of safety. Once you get to the source, you can take action that will reassure people it is safe to say what's on their minds.

Ignoring difficult or controversial issues

If your meetings aren't lively and igniting some controversy, there is probably a lot going unsaid. Avoiding the tough conversations only increases the odds that the team will derail because it is doubtful the real problems are being addressed. High-performing teams are willing to tackle the difficult issues. They know that working through them and coming to alignment keeps the team on track. If you are the leader, you need to draw out the difficult and controversial issues, not suppress them.

Not giving strong direction

Ambiguity is dangerous. Better for a team to occasionally miss a deadline than not to have one at all. Be sure that all of your goals and action items are clear.

Blaming

When things go wrong or a mistake is made, it's easy to cast blame rather than take responsibility. This behavior is symptomatic of many potential problems—lack of accountability, lack of trust, and lack of process to name a few. The leader can set a clear norm that discourages this type of behavior. Ideally, the team should learn from its mistakes and failures by having an assessment and feedback process that objectively looks at what worked and what didn't.

Criticizing

Feedback given in a critical way can be hurtful or humiliating to a team member. It also tends to be unproductive. Criticism delivered without thinking in the heat of the moment is likely only to provoke defensiveness and discouragement. Constructive feedback, which is imperative for a team to function at peak levels, is always served with compassion, specificity about the behavior to be changed, and suggestions for what the new behavior needs to be. Make constructive feedback a team norm.

Withdrawing

When a team member withdraws from participating, it is a sign that something is amiss. Withdrawing is often a response to not feeling valued or heard. It is important for all team members to participate and contribute. Be sure that the team establishes the norm that everyone is responsible for the full participation of the entire team. If you are a team member and notice people are not speaking out, be sure to draw them out.

Chronic complaining

An occasional complaint is normal. Chronic complaining is symptomatic of other problems—lack of alignment, lack of resources, lack of communication, lack of support. Clear problem-solving and decision-making procedures will alleviate much of it. But pay attention to the specific complaints to get to the source of the problem. Teams that can channel complaints into requests, and ultimately action, are more likely to be successful.

Establish Norms

To be a high-functioning team, you should identify explicit norms and encourage behaviors and attitudes that spur greater performance. We define norms as standards of conduct to which all members subscribe. These norms should be articulated early in the formation of your team. This is especially important for cross-functional teams, since the norms members bring from their individual functional groups must be integrated or replaced by different norms.

Norms can cover both structural and interpersonal issues. Structural issues include the establishment of rewards and consequences, how responsibility is assigned and accepted, how progress or status is reported, how feedback is provided, and the frequency, agenda, and process of meetings. Your team can also identify interpersonal behaviors such as the need for truth telling, how members encourage and/or compete with each other, how conflict is handled, what attitudes are sought and—very important—how destructive behavior is identified and stopped.

Some of the issues mentioned above are also discussed in other chapters. Here, we are emphasizing the advantage of formally and explicitly describing your team's norms. The highest functioning teams develop norms together rather than the leader establishing the norms. A team that can agree on their standards of behavior is more likely to enforce them and hold each other accountable for doing what they say.

High-functioning teams also operate with an important norm governing team membership. Frequently team members do not volunteer to be part of a cross-functional team. They are assigned by their functional management. In many instances, those who are assigned may not be the best match for the team. It may be that they do not have the necessary skills, do not have the time to devote to the project, or do not see any personal advantage in being part of the team. Or perhaps they do not identify with the team or subscribe to its other norms. Very often teams are stymied by the assumption that members cannot be removed if they were assigned by functional organization. They make the costly mistake of tolerating even highly destructive members on the team. When your team has a norm or standard for membership, however, you have a basis to include or exclude members.

One final word on norms and team identity: Fundamental to your team's identity are the characteristics which will lead your team to success. Norms are a way your team can faithfully exhibit them. Whatever the characteristic, such as resiliency, flexibility, endurance, innovation, attention, skill or craft, norms make clear the attitudes and behaviors required and make them active and alive on your team.

Select actions from the list below that you want your team to act on. Add other actions as you see necessary.

Success Factor Actions:

	YES	NO	DONE
Define the norms by which your team will operate.	☐	☐	☐
Devise a way to measure how well your team exhibits its norms and behaviors.	☐	☐	☐
Define how to correct counterproductive behaviors.	☐	☐	☐
Correct behaviors that are counterproductive.	☐	☐	☐
Determine how membership will be confirmed.	☐	☐	☐
Other:			
	☐	☐	☐
	☐	☐	☐

THE PLAN FACTOR

What a member of a high-performing team observes:
  Our team has a clear plan that will get us to our goals.
  I know how my roles and responsibilities fit into the team's plan.
  I am committed to the purpose and goals of the team.

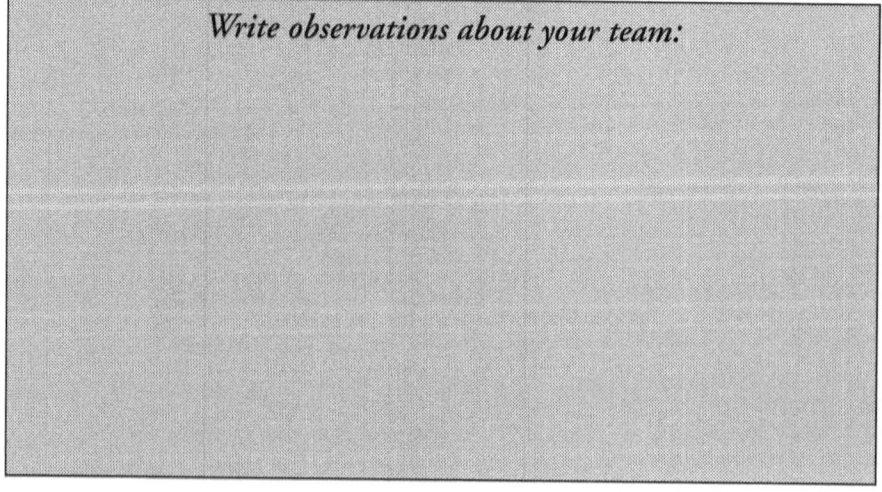

Write observations about your team:

The Coach's Perspective

Creating a shared purpose and plan is the hallmark of a high-performing cross-functional team. Low-performing teams either lack a clear purpose and plan or are not aligned to them. These shortcomings set the team on a path to potential failure. Cross-functional teams can be particularly vulnerable, since the members come from different functional organizations with their own plans and agendas.

Your team's ability to succeed is built upon the business framework that your plan and purpose provide. While your identity asserts who your team is, your purpose states what your team will accomplish. With a well-articulated purpose, your team will further unite your members to serve and produce value for your customers and stakeholders.

Plans that are developed by all the members of a team have the highest probability of success. When each member contributes to the "what, when, and how" things will be done, you will have more individual and collective ownership of the plan. In this scenario, it's very likely that all your members will buy into or believe in the plan. It's important that all of the members know how they fit in, how they will contribute to the plan, and the scope of their responsibilities. Clear roles and responsibilities reduce redundancy and conflict while promoting efficiency and job satisfaction.

A successful team's action plan will include the following:

- A description of the overall result that is expected and why it is important to accomplish it (business impact, customer value, competitive response, regulatory or legal imperative)
- A statement of the desired result, or goal, the target date for achieving it, and the measures of success to be used
- A list of sub-goals with target dates for achievement and the accountable team members specified

- A list of specific steps to be taken, by whom and by when, for each sub-goal

- Activity and goal dependencies

- Key milestones for success

It must also specify:

- The resources that are required, including people and dollars

- How, when, and to whom progress will be reported

- How the plan will be updated to reflect progress and changing business conditions

The plan then becomes a document to be used for discussion with and buy-in of functional organizations that are providing resources to the initiative.

Sometimes a team will be given its plan and objectives by its sponsor. When this occurs, it is important for the leader to build alignment among the members to the plan. Even when everyone does not completely agree or like the objectives, you must find a way that all team members can give the plan their support and gather the resources needed. They don't have to agree with everything, but they need to align with the general plan and be committed to their specific areas of accountability. Communicating the background and business conditions driving the project will help each member to get on board quickly. A good leader will anticipate some push back and quickly spot passive resistance, indifference, and outright opposition. If a team member is undermining the effort or creating active opposition, this must be dealt with. Simply, the member must change their position or be transferred from the team.

Select actions from the list below that you want your team to act on.
Add other actions as you see necessary.

Success Factor Actions:

	YES	NO	DONE
Engage your team to produce a plan of action.	☐	☐	☐
Clearly and concisely define the purpose of your team.	☐	☐	☐
Be sure all team members support the team's purpose.	☐	☐	☐
Define a plan that includes tasks, dependencies, and schedules.	☐	☐	☐
Confirm that all team members are aligned and committed to the final plan.	☐	☐	☐
Other:			
	☐	☐	☐
	☐	☐	☐

THE PROCESS FACTOR

HOW EFFECTIVELY DOES THE TEAM COMMUNICATE AND
MAKE DECISIONS?

What a member of a high-performing team observes:

I see a high level of truthfulness and openness among members of the team.

The team has effective ways of communicating.

The team has an effective decision-making process that is backed by functional management.

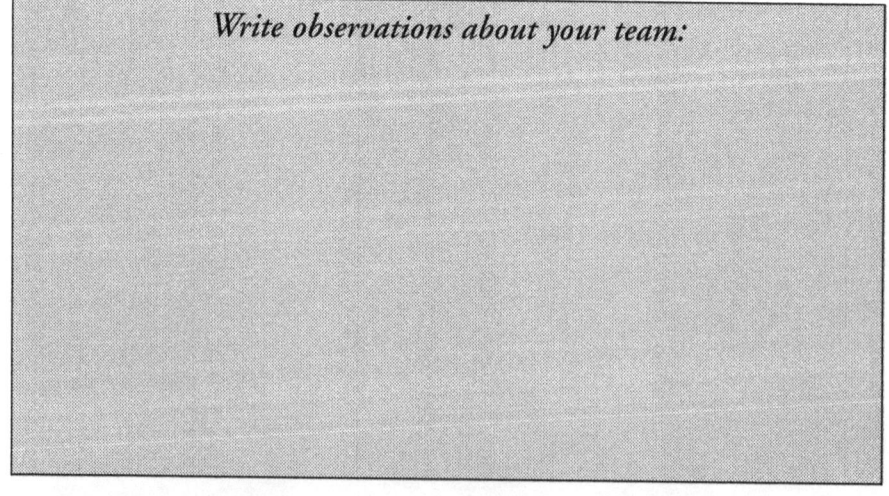

Write observations about your team:

The Coach's Perspective

Cross-functional teams face special complexities that require excellent communication and decision processes. Members and resources are often distributed in many places, possibly continents apart. The team must meld multiple chains of command. Decision-making responsibilities and procedures may not be standard. For example, the team may operate across levels or even in an inverted structure. This may mean that members at different levels must collaborate as peers, or that higher level members will sometimes report to lower level members. These conditions require a high level of trust among all of the team members.

Dysfunctional teams fail to adapt to these complexities. With insufficient communication, misunderstanding, confusion, conflict, and distrust grow; critical information is not received; and alignment never happens. Without a clear decision-making process, decisions never become final or are not accepted. Under these conditions, progress is almost impossible.

Bridging The Complexities

The most successful cross-functional teams bridge the complexities they face. They focus on creating trust, fostering open communication, and developing an effective decision-making process.

Trust

Cross-functional teams must establish trust among members early on. Trust is built through developing relationships based on mutual understanding. A team that operates with a high degree of trust feels safe to discuss anything, including controversial issues. Your members must be able to ask for help when plans go off track or when they encounter roadblocks or obstacles. When your team operates with a foundation of trust, you will have more open dialogue and debate. Truthfulness becomes the norm.

Trust is developed by successfully doing four things:

- getting to know each other's abilities and skills

- keeping commitments

- communicating frequently and honestly

- knowing and acting in each other's best interests

In a unified team, members have confidence in each other's abilities. To achieve this, a team begins by taking stock of everyone's strengths. Next, this inventory of skills is mapped to what is required for your team to succeed. Your planning can then utilize the collective strengths of your team and take into account any gaps. Confidence naturally results when roles and responsibilities are assigned to competent team members with the skills to do their respective jobs.

Trust is earned when members do what they say—they keep and honor commitments. Your teams will lose trust quickly if members do not keep commitments. Because of the time pressure a cross-functional team is usually under, you must be on the lookout for members over promising. If your team begins to "over promise and under deliver," it is likely to derail. You should create an environment where people can honestly discuss requested deadlines and their feasibility. If someone can't deliver on a commitment, they must feel safe enough to raise a warning flag and ask for help.

A high-performing team acts in the best interests of its members. You can only act on another's best interests when you know what they are. Taking the time in the early stages of the team's formation to get to know each other's values, needs, and interests is essential.

Communication

High-functioning teams rely on effective communication. Your cross-functional team's communication and decision-making processes must be more structured than usual for several reasons. First, a cross-functional team by its very nature is operating outside of standard company and organizational procedures. As the team ramps up, establishing a communication process will insure that people know what's expected and keep everyone informed. Secondly, team members may not all be in the same location, such as in the case of a virtual cross-functional team. Teams that operate virtually especially need structure to be sure that people feel connected and all members are kept "in the loop." Lastly, since cross-functional teams rely less on the informal networks that develop over time, establishing more formal networks is key.

You should specifically assign responsibility for communicating and put regularly scheduled vehicles for doing so into place right away. Vehicles that are easy to use and maintain, such as email and online bulletin boards, are best. Ask members to report progress simply and powerfully through a few key measures. Establish a routine to communicate emergency or exceptional information, including who initiates the report and who is required to respond. It is helpful for team members to provide feedback to the originators about the timeliness, usefulness, and conciseness of their communications.

Decision-Making

High-functioning teams establish the "who, what, when, and how" of their decision process and keep it as simple and actionable as possible. Define the types of decisions to be made, who will be affected by them, and who should participate in making them. Generally there are three approaches from which to choose: consensus, vote, or leader directive. A consensus, of course, generates the greatest participation, since everyone comes to an agreement and supports the final decision. In a team vote, an agreed upon percentage of the members, generally a majority, make the decision. In the third approach the team leader is the sole decision maker and issues a directive. This is particularly useful when an immediate decision must be made during a crisis or if there is a time constraint. All three approaches are useful. The important considerations are the complexity of the decision, the people it will affect, and the time constraints. Recognize that conditions may call for the team to switch approaches. In extreme circumstances, the leader may need to override a decision reached by consensus or vote. It will benefit the team to discuss and understand these exceptional situations and how they will be handled.

Most cross-functional teams need to keep functional management informed and have approval for their decision-making processes. Not only is it inefficient to come to decisions that may be overturned by functional management, but it undermines a team's morale and sense of empowerment. Once your team has agreed upon its decision-making processes, share them with functional management. This dialogue will allow the team to understand the scope and boundaries of its decision-making power.

Situations may arise, however, where involving functional management in the decision-making process is unnecessary or is to be avoided. Perhaps, for example, a team has been formed to solve a problem that the cross-functional organizations can't agree on. In this situation, the team sponsor must make clear the teams' decision-making authority.

It's also important for team members to know when they have enough data to make a decision. Many teams become paralyzed by the need for certainty in their decisions. Great teams pride themselves on being able to get behind decisions even when they are not 100% sure if the decision is correct. A strong leader will know when the time has come to decide and will effectively move the team in that direction.

Select actions from the list below that you want your team to act on. Add other actions as you see necessary.

Success Factor Actions:	YES	NO	DONE
Create norms for how communication will take place among your members	☐	☐	☐
Create communications vehicles for your team	☐	☐	☐
Create an exception-reporting process	☐	☐	☐
Create and implement a decision-making process that is backed by functional management	☐	☐	☐
Decide what strengths, skills, and abilities are needed for your team to be successful	☐	☐	☐
Inventory the team to assess strength and gaps	☐	☐	☐
Establish truthfulness as a team norm	☐	☐	☐
Other:			
	☐	☐	☐
	☐	☐	☐

THE FUNCTIONAL FACTOR

HOW ARE THE TEAM'S EFFORTS INTEGRATED INTO THE
FUNCTIONAL ORGANIZATIONS?

What a member of a high-performing team observes:

My functional management is aligned with my team roles and responsibilities.

My functional budget includes the needs of the team.

My functional management acknowledges and rewards my work for the team.

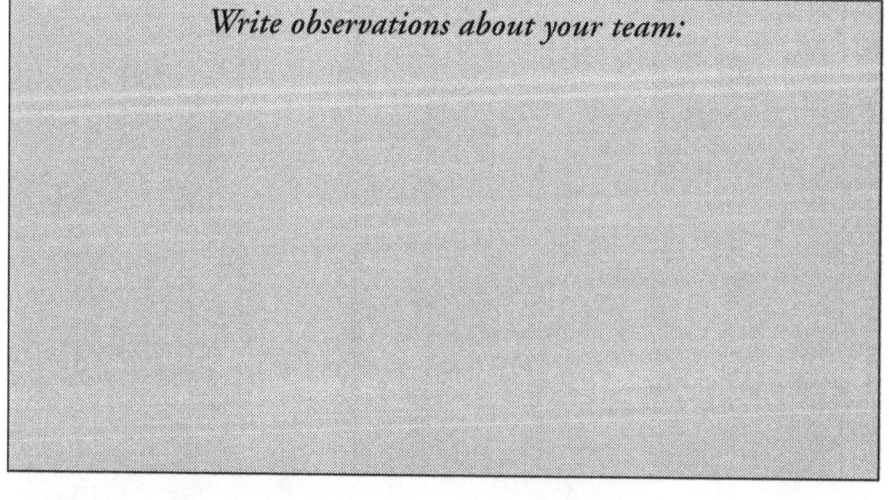

Write observations about your team:

The Coach's Perspective

Cross-functional teams are designed to overcome the organizational barriers that exist between functional organizations. When a team simply assumes that key functional stakeholders understand and are aligned on its purpose, goals, and plan, it can lead to less than stellar results, because the barriers will still be there. A highly functioning team recognizes that success comes from fully integrating their work into each functional organization. You can accomplish this in a number of ways.

Integrating Your Work

Your team can ensure that everyone is aligned and educate everyone about the purpose, goals, and action plan of the team. Sponsorship of your team is resolved at the start of the initiative. An effective decision-making process backed by the represented functional organizations should be agreed upon early on. Your team should communicate regularly with the functional organizations to ensure that the required functional budgets and resources are allocated. This important step is often overlooked and the team finds itself without the resources to do the job.

The team leader cannot assume that the assigned members work for the team full time. Normally, functional groups volunteer their people to participate as time permits while they continue to do their "regular full-time" jobs. As part of the alignment process, your members' roles and responsibilities and time commitments must be clearly defined with each functional organization.

A cross-functional team leader can be the catalyst to insure that everyone's work is valued and understood. Formal feedback and acknowledgment are extremely important. A strong team leader will give performance feedback directly to the management of each functional organization to ensure that both individual and team contributions are recognized.

Overcoming Barriers

Your team may encounter organizational barriers. Some barriers to anticipate are:

Political battles between organizations. It's very possible that alignment cannot be reached because of in-fighting between one or more functional organizations. When one functional organization makes a power play, the needs of the business and focus on the customer can get lost. Alliances with other organizations can generate influence to keep the team's business focus.

Rigid hierarchies. Breaking through these long-standing structures can be daunting. Understanding how the informal network operates and plugging into it can help.

A lack of organizational passion for the project. Sometimes a project initiated by one organization just doesn't make it onto the radar screen of other groups. In this case, the leader can gain alignment by learning more about other functional priorities and how this project might benefit them. Reinforcing the business and customer value to be gained, and linking it to functional priorities, will also help to create more excitement and support.

Inertia. Some functional organizations may have a hard time letting go of deeply embedded and long-standing policies and processes. The leader will need to work with senior functional leadership to gain their support to make changes.

The existence of barriers is often the reason a cross-functional team was formed in the first place. The challenge for the team is to overcome them. There may be times when these barriers cannot be overcome and the team must operate outside the approval of the functional organizations. If this is the case, the team needs to get support from the sponsor to work independently and out of process.

Select actions from the list below that you want your team to act on. Add other actions as you see necessary.

Success Factor Actions:	YES	NO	DONE
Communicate the team's plan to functional management.	☐	☐	☐
Align functional management to members' responsibilities.	☐	☐	☐
Make sure functional budgets contain the resources the team requires.	☐	☐	☐
Have functional management include team feedback in members' performance review.	☐	☐	☐
Other:			
	☐	☐	☐
	☐	☐	☐

THE FEEDBACK FACTOR

HOW IS THE PERFORMANCE OF THE TEAM AND ITS MEMBERS EVALUATED AND REWARDED?

What a member of a high-performing team observes:
The team evaluates its performance regularly.
I get regular feedback from the team on my performance.

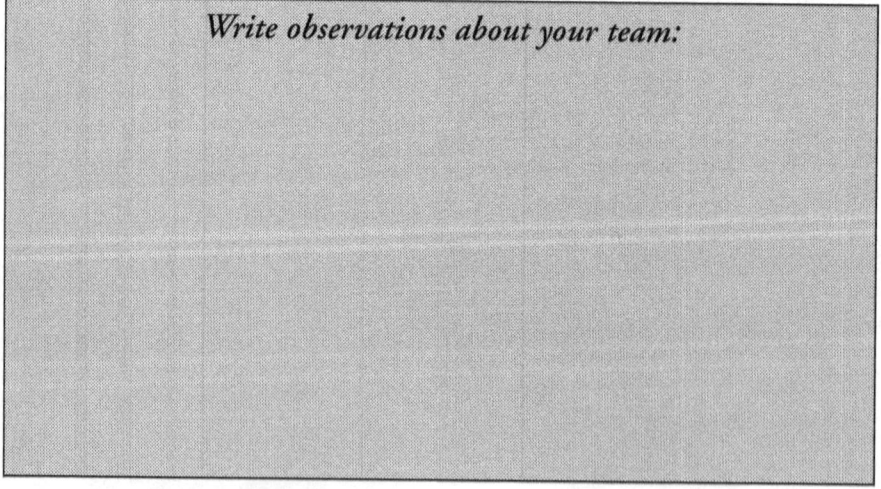

Write observations about your team:

The Coach's Perspective

Many cross-functional teams function without a way to evaluate and reward the work of the team and its individual team members. This often leads to a lack of motivation. Team members lose focus if they

feel their work is not appreciated or recognized, or if their performance has no effect on their standing in their home organizations.
High-functioning teams maintain focus and motivation by evaluating
and rewarding individual and team performance.

Evaluating Performance

An effective team leader recognizes the necessity and importance of
evaluating individual and team performance. Several things must be
considered: (1) what to evaluate, (2) who to get feedback from, (3)
the frequency of feedback, (4) what process to use, (5) how to link
individual performance to team performance, and (6) how to link
performance to each member's functional organization.

It's important to choose evaluation criteria, or measures of success,
that are meaningful and linked to the team's goals. Depending on the
nature of the team's work, a team may opt to evaluate project timeliness, budgets, cost savings, productivity improvements, revenue
generation, or customer satisfaction. Key deliverables and measures
of success linked to the team's plan are the most effective ways to
track and evaluate the progress of both the team and individual
members. The team should consider evaluating how they are doing,
collectively and individually, relative to team norms.

Evaluations should be done frequently enough to catch problems
early, keep things on track, and keep everyone informed. Feedback
on individual and team performance can come from a variety of
sources—the team itself, customers, the team sponsor, and each
member's functional organization. An effective team leader will
incorporate a way to obtain feedback on individual and team performance from the stakeholders of the team.

Creating an evaluation process insures that everyone understands what will be evaluated, by whom, and when. The process can be done face to face or by written report and either individually or as a team. Feedback reports can be quite effective if they are well thought out and designed. A strong team leader can be the catalyst, insuring that everyone's work is valued both by the team and by members' functional organizations.

Recognizing and Rewarding Performance

With an evaluation process in place, it becomes equally important for the team to reward and recognize individual and team success. This can be done both formally and informally. Formal guidelines can be developed specifying what will be rewarded and what rewards will be given. A budget should be established for rewards. A formalized rewards process can stand alone or be linked to each functional organization's process. This linkage maximizes the rewards individuals receive for their contributions.

It's important that small successes be recognized as well as larger ones. This can be done through informal means, such as a simple "thank you" for a job well done or an acknowledgment of the impact someone has had on the team. You can recognize a team member's positive attitude, flexibility, or personal initiative, for example, or express appreciation that someone has gone above and beyond what was expected. Timely recognition no matter how informal is always appreciated by the recipient.

Celebrating when key milestones are reached or objectives accomplished is a great way to keep morale high. When recognition comes from many different places—the team leader, team members, functional management, and customers—it has the greatest impact. Team celebrations reinforce the team's identity and sense of cohesiveness.

Select actions from the list below that you want your team to act on. Add other actions as you see necessary.

Success Factor Actions:

	YES	NO	DONE
Develop a rewards plan to reinforce norms and plan of action.	☐	☐	☐
Encourage the team to examine its performance regularly.	☐	☐	☐
Provide feedback regarding individual performance regularly.	☐	☐	☐
Reward individual and team performance regularly.	☐	☐	☐
Link performance rewards to functional organizations.	☐	☐	☐
Other:			
	☐	☐	☐
	☐	☐	☐

THE RESPONSIBILITY FACTOR

WHAT LEVEL OF RESPONSIBILITY AND COMMITMENT DO MEMBERS OF THE TEAM DEMONSTRATE?

What a member of a high-performing team observes:

Team members deliver on their responsibilities to the team.

I am committed to this team.

I see a level of commitment from the other members of the team.

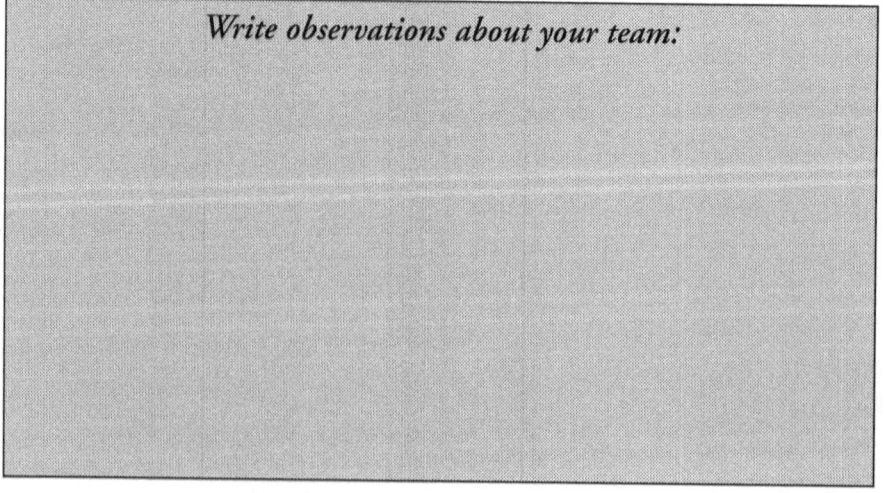

Write observations about your team:

The Coach's Perspective

Cross-functional teams are groupings of individuals whose combined talents and efforts produce something that the sum of their individual functional work would not. Commitment and responsibility are the fuel that propel the action and progress of the team. When members are committed to the team's purpose, the team will deliver the potential inherent in a cross-functional team. Commitment and responsibility are built upon engagement and will come more readily for a team with engaged members. Commitment and responsibility are the fruits of the effort put into building engagement.

But what does commitment mean for a cross-functional team? The American Heritage dictionary defines commitment as "a pledge to do something," or "the state of being bound emotionally or intellectually to a course of action." Fundamentally, when people commit they are choosing to participate in something, which implies that either desire and/or willingness are present. Our definition of commitment for cross-functional teams is "choosing to participate in achieving the team's purpose with wholehearted intention." A hallmark of commitment is when members take full responsibility for their actions and their results.

Lack of commitment and responsibility plagues teams that don't produce. The symptoms are readily seen. Members balancing multiple responsibilities can be distracted. The assignment of roles and responsibilities is unclear. Agreements are not in place or are vague. There is inconsistent follow-through. Deadlines are missed and things start to fall behind. Team members are easily stymied by setbacks or resistance.

Getting Commitment and Taking Responsibility

The high-functioning team ensures that commitment is in place. This means that each member chooses to give their best work to the team. When the team develops its plan, roles and responsibilities are made clear. Team members show commitment when they accept their responsibilities with confidence and give their assurances that they will deliver.

Creating commitment is not only the team leader's job. Everyone on the team is involved. The team should pay attention to how responsibilities are assigned and accepted. You can bring the power of the team to bear by creating a formal process in which the whole team participates. Members can be asked to declare to the team their acceptance of and commitment to their responsibilities. This approach is especially warranted when there is significant interdependency among team members.

High-functioning teams establish norms that support responsibility and commitment to the team. It should always be valued when members define and accept their own responsibility. Team members are expected to give their best or to communicate when they cannot. If a responsibility cannot be met, your members should inform the team early enough so that adjustments can be made. It is acceptable for your members to acknowledge when someone is not "pulling their own weight" and offer support. When members admit that problems exist, your team can resolve any lack of aligned responsibility. Persistence and tenacity should be commended. Encourage internal attitudes that foster responsibility.

Having responsibility is a personal challenge that individual team members must master. Your own sense of responsibility drives you to achieve your goals. When you have responsibility, you know it is up to you to get by any impasse and to resolve any dilemma. You do not sidestep, deflect, or deny when the inevitable changes, missteps, and downright errors happen, whether they are caused by you or others. Having responsibility is having personal initiative.

When you take responsibility on a team, you are saying many things. You are saying that its success rests with you. You are saying that you have the necessary resources and are confident that you will carry it off. You are pledging that you will totally manage it by planning, anticipating, and taking immediate action when necessary. You will track your progress and not only raise issues but also lead construc-tive responses.

An individual member's lack of responsibility is an issue for the entire team. When individual members fail to deliver, it jeopardizes the results of the team. If the team used the recommended team-wide process for accepting and committing to responsibilities, the team has set the stage to utilize a powerful tool to affect the behav-ior of non-delivering members. These members should be asked to report out and participate in the discussion of how the teams deal with the shortfall so that progress can continue. The goal is not to relieve individuals of their responsibility but rather to keep things on track. This approach works with teams that have created a strong foundation through the team's identity, plan, behaviors, and engagement.

Select actions from the list below that you want your team to act on.
Add additional actions as you see necessary.

Success Factor Actions:

	YES	NO	DONE
Be sure members are aligned on values, norms, and objectives.	☐	☐	☐
Implement a formal process for team commitment.	☐	☐	☐
Be sure members have ownership of their responsibilities.	☐	☐	☐
If commitments are missed, ensure that impacts are understood.	☐	☐	☐
Give members the chance to define their responsibilities.	☐	☐	☐
Establish norms that support commitment and responsibility.	☐	☐	☐
Other:			
	☐	☐	☐
	☐	☐	☐

THE SELF-INTEREST FACTOR

DO THE TEAM MEMBERS SEE PERSONAL ADVANTAGES TO WORKING ON THE TEAM?

What a member of a high-performing team observes:
   I value the personal payoffs I get from being on this team.
   I am proud of my contribution to this team.

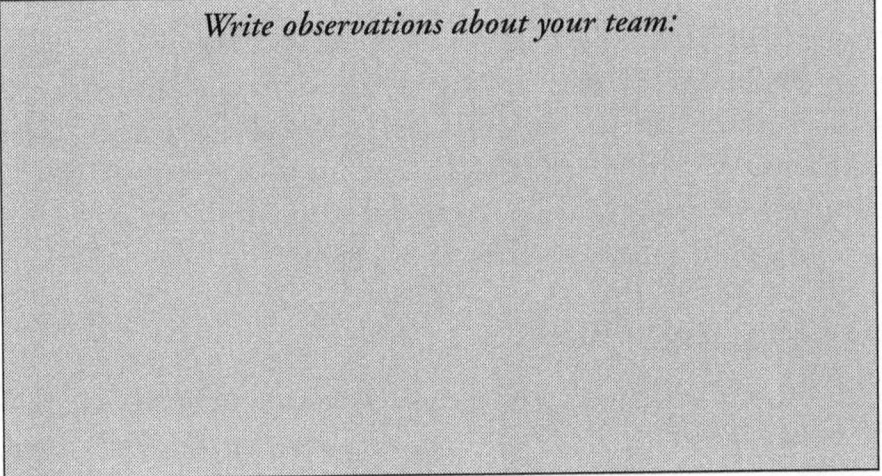

Write observations about your team:

The Coach's Perspective

Self-interest is a powerful motivator. When a team doesn't serve its members' interests, it struggles to accomplish its goals or get results.

If the team members' passion and aspirations are not engaged, their teams will not get the most from them.

A high-functioning team recognizes that when individual team members see personal advantages to working on a team they are more highly motivated. They use more of their natural talents on the work of the team.

What do we mean by personal advantages? It's the answer each member would give to the question, "What's in it for me?" or "What do I gain as a result of participating?" It might be the opportunity to grow skills, use your talents, increase your visibility, work on an interesting project or work with people you enjoy. It will be different for each person.

Strong team leaders take the time to explore with members the personal advantages that participating on the team could give them. If your members do not perceive any personal advantages, their engagement will be minimal. Ultimately, it may be better to replace members who see no benefit. The best standard is that every member gain personal advantage from being on your team.

Identifying Personal Payoffs

Do not assume that every team member will know or be able to readily define what is important to them. Very often members will come onto the team with more questions about the value of their participation than answers. Providing them answers quickly however can miss the mark and fail to motivate them in a positive way. The first step, before listing the advantages the team provides, all of which they may see as irrelevant, is to investigate with the members what is important to them.

Personal Values

Exploring personal values is a quick and effective technique to help you and the member get to underlying motivators. Values can be revealed in a number of ways, whether in a conversation or in a questionnaire. In either case, the critical elements are the questions asked and the honesty of the answers given. Because honesty is based on trust, a good approach is to let team members decide if they want to do this exploration with help, such as in conversation, or on their own. In either case, here is a list of questions we use as coaches to help people identify more clearly what they value.

What must I have in my life at work?

What makes me the happiest?

What do I need to feel fulfilled?

When was I the happiest or most fulfilled in my life? What was valuable at that time to me?

What is most important to me in my life?

What is most important about me that I want other people to know?

What do I want? What do I yearn for?

If my life were perfect, what would it look like?

What gets my juices flowing?

What is present when I am at my best?

What would be present if I were being who I truly am?

Through these inquiries, you can come to a good understanding of what someone values. It is important to remember that these values are deeply personal. By starting with a broader life perspective, rather than asking questions that are directly work-related, you will gain more insight into the motivation and satisfaction a person finds—or needs—on the job.

Here is a list of characteristics, ideals, and experiences that people value:

Humor	Directness	Partnership
Productivity	Service	Contribution
Excellence	Independence	Focus
Romance	Recognition	Harmony
Accomplishment	Orderliness	Honesty
Zest	Success	Adventure
Tradition	Authenticity	Growth
Aesthetics	Relationship	Participation
Performance	Collaboration	Community
Personal Power	Freedom	Connectedness
Acknowledgment	Comradeship	Lightness
Spirituality	Self-Expression	Integrity
Creativity	Innovation	Uniqueness
Nurturing	Joy	Beauty
Peace	Elegance	Trust

Once a team member's values are understood, the next step is to relate the person's values to the possibilities that participating on the team will create. A powerful way to accomplish this is for members to identify the relationships between what they value and what they might gain from being on the team themselves. The leader or other members should verify that the connections are valid. Simply, there must be reality behind how people believe their aspiration will be satisfied on the team. For example, a person who values innovation may be asked to participate in activities that require new thinking, ideas, and creativity. While this would not be the team member's primary function, it would allow for their value of innovation to be expressed as part of the team.

Personal Strengths

Often, the most direct benefit for members is simply the chance to do something that they are good at. There is great satisfaction in doing a job well. Having the chance to use their personal strengths can be a major payoff for members of a cross-functional team.

Your challenge is to recognize your members' strengths no matter where they may lie. There is a spectrum of categories, all of which can be useful to the team. Strengths can be soft skills, such as empathy; personal characteristics, such as resilience; technical expertise, such as the ability to create spread sheets; or self-forged resources, such as a useful network of contacts across the firm.

While your recognition of team members' strengths is a boost in itself, the real payoff comes when their strengths are used effectively in the work of the team. For example, when someone who has empathy and great communicating skills is asked to be the customer interface, both the team and the individual member will benefit from these strengths. The payoff is more than a win-win. You have greatly increased the likelihood of success for both the individual and the team when the person most gifted to perform a task does so.

Cross-functional teams can also serve members' interests by helping them recognize their talents and abilities. We recommend taking and sharing assessments such as the Myers Briggs Personality Type Indicator and Gallup's Strengths Finder Profile, which can be engaging ways for members to learn more about themselves and each other. Being on a cross-functional team often gives members the chance to do new things, to experiment, and to discover new abilities. When you help people reassess and expand their potential, you are giving them a big payoff.

Select actions from the list below that you want your team to act on. Add other actions as you see necessary.

Success Factor Actions:	YES	NO	DONE
Ask members to identify their values.	☐	☐	☐
Ask members to identify the advantages of being on the team.	☐	☐	☐
Determine how each member can gain their benefits.	☐	☐	☐
Engage the team to help each member gain their benefits.	☐	☐	☐
Other:			
	☐	☐	☐
	☐	☐	☐

Conclusion

The People Element

Your cross-functional team has the potential to create extraordinary value for your company. It can deliver results that the normal functional organization could not. Your team can overcome organizational barriers to create new solutions that were not available before. Your team can be more effective in a shorter time frame. All of this is possible if your team handles the challenges of a cross-functional team.

Many of the difficulties your team will face could be present anytime a team is formed. But they are heightened in a cross-functional setting, because time horizons are compressed, expectations are raised, and the interests of many chains of command must be integrated. Yet, remarkably, underlying all of these demands is the basic fact that a group of people can bring themselves together in such a way that their individual and collective performances are enhanced by their being a team.

When you look back at the ten critical factors we have covered in this book and the considerations that we stressed for each one, you will see again and again that our emphasis is on the people of the team. We asked you to focus above all on how to unite your team and how to ensure that each member is engaged and maximally contributing.

This is the result of our experience either directly managing or coaching a multitude of cross-functional teams. We saw with many different situations and approaches what worked and what didn't.

We learned that for team success, the key element is the human element. From our experience, we can wholeheartedly assert that when teams focus on the human element, they are more likely to be successful. Why is this? The bottom line is that people are what make the team work and generate results. When your team calls forth and focuses the potential of its members, it will fulfill its inherent potential and produce the best results possible, no matter how difficult and dynamic the conditions you face.

We also learned that there are both more and less successful ways of focusing on the people element. We have experience with a wide range of approaches from total prescription to full participation. We have observed that while prescription produces results it does so with less passion and greater effort by all. The leader works harder to motivate and must become the watchdog to enforce the rules. With full participation, each member's motivation is self generated and the team abides by norms and behaviors agreed to by all. The members are more self-governing. Fundamentally, we observed that different approaches produced different attitudes and behaviors, which in turn determined the quality of the teams' results.

The path we have laid out for you will expand the value your team creates by expanding the value-creating capacity of its people. In this method, your team recognizes the potential and capacities of your members; engages them in a process of identification with the team's purpose; and involves them in planning the work. Your team will achieve great results when the team is committed to contributing the greatest value to the company and to each member. This commitment will form a foundation, fueling daily motivation, day to day decisions, and forward-thinking plans.

When you call forth the right attitudes and behaviors from your team, you will have many positive experiences. You will experience esprit de corps. You will experience personal and collective growth. Most of all, you will experience the satisfaction of producing the best results your team was capable of producing. Enjoy meeting the challenges and fulfilling the potential of your cross-functional team.

About TRUID

The Enterprise Challenge

Companies today are challenged to constantly increase the value they create to satisfy customers and shareholders. Many companies respond by cutting costs, down-sizing, and improving productivity, often simply by working their people more. While effective in the short run, these actions do little to sustain competitive advantage or margins. Enduring companies, or great companies as we call them, focus their efforts on more than just the short-term bottom line. Great companies expand the value they produce by expanding the value-creating capacity of their people. At TRUID, we are committed to helping companies create greater value through the power of their people's commitment.

The Individual Challenge

People work longer and harder than before yet wonder if their work really matters. The rapid pace of business leaves people feeling disconnected from their families, their colleagues, and their bigger purpose. People keenly feel any disconnection from work because work links their personal development and their contribution to the world. At TRUID, we are committed to helping individuals discover what they value most and what they want to contribute. They reconnect to their passions, purpose, and the relationships that are most important.

The Professionals of TRUID

Emilio De Lia and Ellen Fredericks are certified executive coaches and former Global Fortune 100 corporate executives. After coaching hundreds of leaders, Emilio and Ellen realized that a key element for success was often missing in today's businesses. This was commitment. Current trends in our highly dynamic and competitive world seem to diminish and discourage employee loyalty. Emilio and Ellen see the resurgence of "people first" as the path to maximize value, especially now. They have observed the advantages and benefits when leaders used commitment as the basis for motivation. Their personal experience and success building and leading large teams was rooted in commitment. In TRUID, they are dedicated to helping individuals, leaders, and companies create success through commitment.

Emilio De Lia is co-founder of TRUID. During his 26 years in Fortune 100 companies, he took up numerous challenges to start up, grow, or turn around divisions. As a leader, he put his people at the center of his value equation, and his organizations excelled in growing revenues, profits, and employee and customer satisfaction. He encouraged attitudes of ownership and commitment to heighten performance; relationships to build winning teams; and training to equip his people with hard and soft skills. As an executive coach, clients continually point to his dedication, his business acumen, and his ability to help them fulfill new possibilities. His TRUID work lets him serve leaders, associates, and organizations in their quest to create value and success.

Emilio's philosophy is based on his observation of the "value and joy" people get from their work: "Work is a great place for personal development and fulfillment. At work, we enter relationships and circumstances that make us grow. When I worked with whole-heartedness, I stretched and learned more than I ever imagined about myself and the world. Through our work, we create lives of substance and value beyond just our livelihood."

Ellen Fredericks, co-founder of TRUID, enjoyed a rich and fulfilling 25-year corporate career prior to becoming an executive coach. As a corporate executive, Ellen led start-up, growth and turnaround initiatives that resulted in increased revenue and profits, and improved productivity. Her strategy for producing results centered on creating a work environment where people felt accountable, acknowledged, committed, and empowered. Her success was also grounded in building and fostering a strong network of business and professional relationships.

Ellen's educational journey earned her a BS in Computer Science, an MS in Management, and a certificate in Coaching. Her corporate journey in the telecommunications industry led her across diverse functional areas such as information technology, operations, marketing, sales, business development, government affairs, and human resources. Her passion for leading large teams and mentoring others led to her professional career in coaching; she is now a Master Certified Coach.

The TRUID Approach

Wholehearted allegiance—commitment—to self and to company creates the greatest value possible. For the individual, that value may be fulfillment, meaning, success, and wealth. For the enterprise, value includes what it creates for its customers, its competitive advantage, superior performance, and financial well-being. TRUID brings a technology and offerings for building commitment in individuals and throughout your organization. Our technology is designed to unite and align the commitment of individuals to themselves with their commitment to the work of the company.

978-0-595-36835-8
0-595-36835-2